STARS 'N STRIPS
FOREVER

Carl Hentsch

American Quilter's Society
P. O. Box 3290 • Paducah, KY 42002-3290
www.AmericanQuilter.com

Located in Paducah, Kentucky, the American Quilter's Society (AQS) is dedicated to promoting the accomplishments of today's quilters. Through its publications and events, AQS strives to honor today's quiltmakers and their work and to inspire future creativity and innovation in quiltmaking.

Executive Book Editor: Andi Milam Reynolds
Senior Book Editor: Linda Baxter Lasco
Graphic Design: Elaine Wilson
Cover Design: Michael Buckingham
Quilt Photography: Charles R. Lynch

Additional copies of this book may be ordered from the American Quilter's Society, PO Box 3290, Paducah, KY 42002-3290, or online at www.AmericanQuilter.com.

Library of Congress Cataloging-in-Publication Data

Hentsch, Carl.
  Stars 'n strips forever / by Carl Hentsch.
    p. cm.
  Summary: "Make a dynamic design by merging two traditional blocks, Rail Fence and Lemoyne Star to create the Stars 'N Strips Block. Vary the number of fabrics used or change their placement to create a limitless number of blocks. Ten projects perfect for the confident beginner and will satisfy the desire to grow for intermediate and advanced stitchers"--Provided by publisher.
  ISBN 978-1-60460-052-0
  1. Patchwork--Patterns. 2. Quilting. I. Title.
  TT835.H4446 2013
  746.46--dc23
               2012045729

title page: This Way That Way, detail, full quilt on page 52

opposite: Mojave Sunset, detail, full quilt on page 40

Dedicated to the innovators.

Acknowledgments

I would like to start by thanking Elaine Johnson from Harper's Fabric & Quilt Co. in Overland Park, Kansas. Hers was one of the first quilt shops that I visited in the area and I always felt welcome there. Elaine has given me guidance and advice and has encouraged me to reach my potential. She was the first shop owner to take the chance to let me teach. Thank you to all the Harper's Girls!

Thanks to Kathy Runyan of I Heart Tula Pink (formerly The Quilt Shoppe) in Stewartsville, Missouri, and Tula Pink. They have encouraged me to grow in my craft, allowed me to assist in the shop, and have provided me with great discounts. I also thank Tula for her friendship, inspiration, and guidance.

Thanks to Janiece Cline and Jeanne Zyck for the wonderful quilting that has completed my quilts; the ladies of the Piece Corps Quilters Guild in Saint Joseph, Missouri, for welcoming me into the guild and for the opportunity to teach and to share my craft with them; and the many other quilt shops throughout Kansas and Missouri that I often visit.

Contents

opposite: Morning Glory, detail, full quilt on page 66

The Adventure Begins

My first quilt design was called SUPER NOVA, and it was juried into the AQS show in Knoxville.

To make sure that wasn't a fluke, I redesigned the quilt as ANEMONE, which hung at the AQS show in Des Moines. It was during this show that I presented this book idea to AQS's executive book editor.

left: SUPER NOVA, 60" x 60" made by the author, quilted by Janiece Cline, Henderson, Nevada (*pattern not included*)

opposite: ANEMONE, 60" x 60" made by the author, quilted by Janiece Cline, Henderson, Nevada (*pattern not included*)

My next attempt was for the 2010 Hoffman Challenge where I created LOVE-ME-KNOT. I was fortunate enough that this quilt made one of the traveling trunk shows and it has been exhibited at the International Quilt Market in Houston.

While at some of the quilt shows, many people asked if patterns were available for my designs, so I decided to start up my quilt pattern company, 3 Dog Design Company. I have published patterns for purchase using this brand. And that brings us to the present day and this book.

I started to design quilts because I wanted to create something that no one else had done. I wanted to be original. The idea for the designs presented here came about when I was looking at the LeMoyne Star block. There had to be something that I could do to make it more interesting, but what was it? The idea kind of hit me like that old commercial, "You got your chocolate in my peanut butter." It was the merging together of the Rail Fence block and the LeMoyne (or Eight-Pointed) Star blocks.

Putting the two blocks together, I came up with the Stars 'N Strips block.

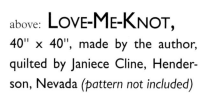

above: LOVE-ME-KNOT, 40" x 40", made by the author, quilted by Janiece Cline, Henderson, Nevada (*pattern not included*)

Stars 'N Strips block

Okay, great, I have this block, how in the world do I piece it? Thankfully, there were many quilters before me who designed ingenious rulers and techniques. I remembered the Fons & Porter™ Half and Quarter Ruler by Omnigrid® that would allow me to cut a triangle with the odd measurements that I needed. Once I figured that out, the rest was "a piece of cake."

I will teach you the technique to make this block in several sizes. We will discover that by simply varying the number of fabrics or their placement, several quilts can be created. I will also teach you a variation on the block and how to make two different quilts using it—CITY NIGHTS (page 56) and MORNING GLORY (page 66). I've also included some great accessories and projects that can be made from the leftover bits and pieces.

Rail Fence block

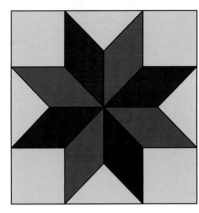

LeMoyne Star block

Stars 'N Strips block

right: **CITRUS PUNCH** table runner, 25½" x 12¾", made by Gina Christensen, Saint Joseph, Missouri

What You'll Need

Fabric Selection

Although I love big prints, they will not work well in these projects. You will be cutting these fabrics into strips, and with a large print, the color will not be consistent. I find that solids, blenders, and small all-over prints work best. Other great choices are cotton satin, shot cottons, small stripes or ikats, and even silks.

Take a look at the CHRISTMAS JEWEL quilt (page 45). It was made with a combination of cotton, dupioni silk, and cotton satin.

NOTE:

Dupioni silk tends to ravel when it is cut. You need to prepare the fabric before cutting. Use a lightweight, fusible interfacing on the wrong side of the fabric to minimize raveling.

MOJAVE (page 31) was made with shot cottons and stripy ikat fabrics.

Batiks for CITRUS PUNCH, page 18

All the projects use three colors, but most of them also use three values within the same colorway. Once you decide on color, pick a light, medium, and dark value in each color.

Basic Supplies

- Rotary cutter and mat
- Fons & Porter™ Half & Quarter Ruler by Omnigrid®
- EasyAngle™ Ruler by Sharon Hultgren
- Rotary ruler with a 45-degree line marked
- Thread
- Iron, ironing board
- Sewing machine in good working order

Cottons, silks, and satins for CHRISTMAS JEWEL, page 45

opposite: CITRUS PUNCH, detail, full quilt on page 18

8" & 12"
Block Construction

It is important to make small test strips and check your seam allowance. This is especially true if you are using anything besides 100-percent quilting-weight cotton. Satins and silks (especially with extra interfacing) will add additional bulk to your piecing. Adjust your needle position if necessary to achieve the correct seam allowance.

I usually cut 6" pieces by the strip width stated in the pattern to make 2 test strip-sets. I press one toward the dark fabrics and one toward the lights. Once I have determined that my strip-sets are the correct width, I write any needle position adjustments that might have been necessary on a small sticky and attach that to the strip-set.

Cutting Diamonds (A Pieces) for the Stars

1. Cut the number of WOF (width-of-fabric) strips as indicated in the pattern.

8" Block	12" Block
1¼" wide strips	1½" wide strips

2. Sew the strips into strip-sets in light, medium, and dark order unless otherwise indicated. Press the seam allowances toward the lighter strips on half the strip-sets and toward the darker strips on the remaining strip-sets.

3. Check the width of your strip-sets and the finished width of the center strip.

8" Block	12" Block
2¾" wide strip-set	3½" wide strip-set
¾" wide center strip	1" wide center strip

4. You will need 4 A pairs for each block. These diamond-shaped pieces are mirror images of each other and are designated A and AR (A reversed).

In order to make cutting easier and quicker, place two strip-sets right sides together. Place the first strip-set on your cutting mat with the darkest strip closest to you. Make sure you always place the strip with the seam allowances pressed toward the dark on the bottom (for the A diamonds). Place a strip-set with the seam allowances pressed toward the light strips on top, again with the darkest fabric closest to you (for the AR diamonds), nestling the seam allowances.

opposite: JULY SPARKLER, detail, full quilt on page 26

5. Align the ruler's 45-degree line on the edge of the fabric or along one of the seam lines. Using a rotary cutter, trim off the end of the fabric.

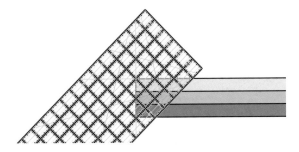

6. Align the 2⅛" or 2¾" line on your ruler with the 45-degree edge of the strip-set. Cut along the ruler for your first shape. Continue cutting the number of diamond segment pairs (A and AR) as specified in your pattern.

8" Block	12" Block
cut 2⅛" wide diamonds	cut 2¾" wide diamonds

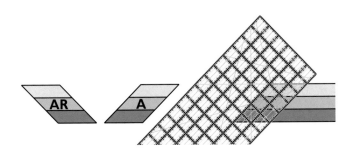

Cutting Triangles for the Squares (B Pieces) and Crosses (C Pieces)

1. Cut the number of WOF strips as indicated in the pattern.

8" Block	12" Block
1" wide strips	1¼" wide strips

2. Sew the strips into strip-sets in light, medium, and dark order unless otherwise indicated. Press the seam allowances on half the strip-sets toward the lighter strips and toward the darker strips on the remaining strip-sets.

> **NOTE:**
> By offsetting each strip by ½" you can cut 1 extra piece from each strip-set.

3. Check the width of your strip-sets and the finished width of the center strip.

8" Block	12" Block
2" wide strip-set	2¾" wide strip-set
½" wide center strip	¾" wide center strip

4. Place 2 strip-sets right sides together. Place the first strip-set on your cutting mat with the darkest strip closest to you. Make sure you always place the strip with the seam allowances pressed toward the dark on the bottom. Place a strip-set with the seam allowances pressed toward the light strips on top, again with the darkest fabric closest to you, nestling the seam allowances.

5. To cut the triangles, line up the line for a 2" or 2¾" strip with the bottom of the strip-sets.

Make a cut on both sides of the Half & Quarter Ruler. This gives you a B1 or C1 pair with the darkest strip at the base of the cut triangle.

8" Block	12" Block
align 2" strip line	align 2¾" strip line

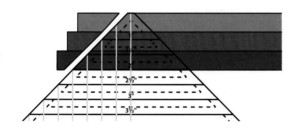

Cutting the B1 or C1 triangles

6. Flip the tool over and line up the 2 or 2¾" line at the top of the strip-set. Make sure that the left side of the ruler is aligned with the previously cut edge. Cut along the opposite edge of the tool. This gives you a B2 or C2 pair with the lightest strip at the base of the cut triangle.

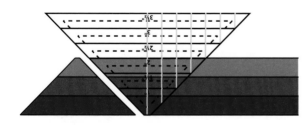

Cutting the B2 or C2 triangles

7. Cut the number of pairs of B and C triangles required by the pattern. You will need one pair EACH B1, B2, C1, and C2 piece for each Stars 'N Strips block.

> **NOTE:**
>
> The A and AR diamonds are mirror images of each other.
>
> The B1 and C1 triangles have the darkest strip across the base.
>
> The B2 and C2 triangles have the lightest strip across the base.

Stars 'N Strips Block Construction

Construction is the same for both the 8" and 12" blocks.

1. Join a C triangle to an A diamond as shown.

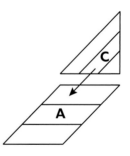

2. Add a B triangle to the AC unit.

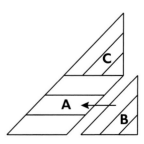

3. Repeat the same process with the other part of the block. You will have a unit that looks like this:

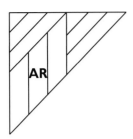

4. Sew these two sections together. This makes one quarter of the block.

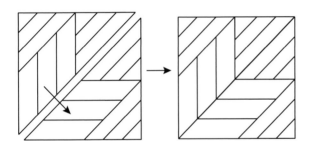

5. Make 3 more quarter units.

6. Measure the sections and, if necessary, square up to measure 4½" x 4½".

8" Block	12" Block
trim to 4½" x 4½"	trim to 6½" x 6½"

7. Lay out the 4 units as shown, sew into pairs, and sew the pairs together to complete the block.

Each project comes with its own block assembly and quilt layout diagrams.

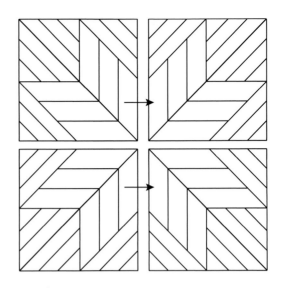

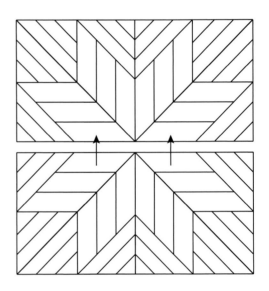

8" Stars 'N Strips Block Projects

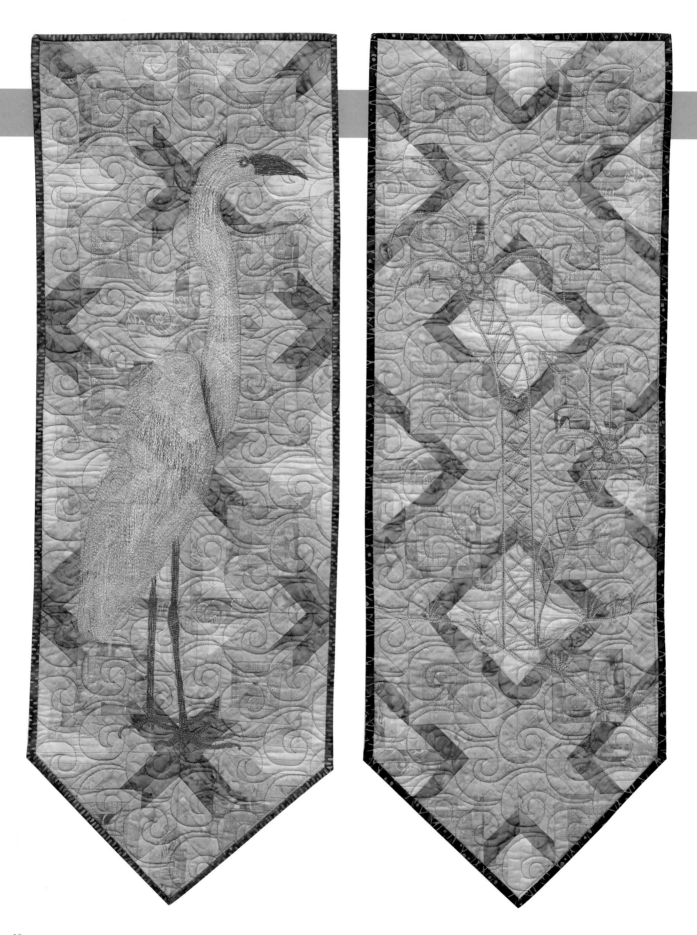

CITRUS PUNCH

Citrus Punch is a great project to start with. It is small and gives you the opportunity to play around with the quilt layout. This wallhanging reminds me of growing up in Florida. I remember going outside to pick oranges every morning for my mother to squeeze.

I chose tone-on-tone batik fabrics for this quilt. The two versions show how easy it is to change the design by simply moving the position of the B or C triangle pairs or by flipping the A so the dark or light is at the center of the star. It is also quite easy to turn this into a table runner or topper by eliminating the corner triangles and making it longer or shorter by adding or deleting a block.

"This table runner was such fun to make. Pressing half of the strip-sets towards the dark and half towards the light, then placing them in pairs, right sides together to cut was strange to me at first. But each set was married perfectly together and made me look like a pro." Gina Christensen, pattern tester

above: **CITRUS PUNCH** table runner, 25½" x 12¾", made by Gina Christensen, Saint Joseph, Missouri

opposite: **CITRUS PUNCH,** both 13" x 38", made by the author, quilted by Janiece Cline, Henderson, Nevada

Fabric Requirements

Group A—for the A & AR diamonds
- ¼ yard light green batik
- ¼ yard medium green batik
- ¼ yard dark green batik

Group B—for the B1 & B2 triangles
- ⅛ yard light orange batik
- ⅛ yard medium orange batik
- ⅛ yard dark orange batik

Group C—for the C1 & C2 triangles
- ⅛ yard light yellow batik
- ⅛ yard medium yellow batik
- ⅛ yard dark yellow batik
- ¼ yard binding
- 17" x 42" batting
- ½ yard backing

Strip-Sets and Cutting

GROUP A

Cut 6 strips 1¼" x WOF from each fabric in Group A.

Sew the strips into strip-sets in dark/medium/ light order.

Following the Block Construction instructions (pages 13–16), cut 22 A/AR pairs.

GROUP B

Cut 4 strips 1" x WOF from each fabric in Group B.

Sew the strips into strip-sets in dark/medium/ light order.

Cut 11 B1 and 11 B2 pairs.

GROUP C

Cut 4 strips 1" x WOF from each fabric in Group C.

Sew the strips into strip-sets in dark/ medium/light order.

Cut 11 C1 and 11 C2 pairs.

Block Assembly

BLOCK 1

Make 3 Block 1 as shown.

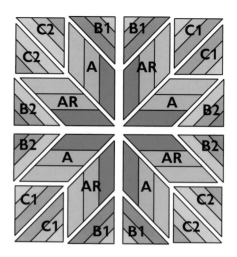

Block 1 assembly

Block 1 — make 3

* * * * * * * * * * *

BLOCK 2

Make 4 Block 2—half blocks for the side setting triangles.

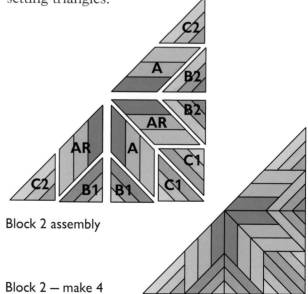

Block 2 assembly

Block 2 — make 4

Block 3

Make 1 Block 3—quarter block for a corner triangle.

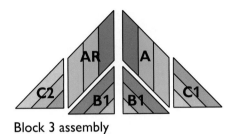

Block 3 assembly

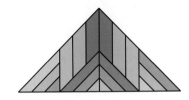

Block 3 — make 1

* * * * * * * * * * * *

Block 4

Make 1 Block 4—quarter block for a corner triangle.

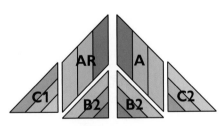

Block 4 assembly

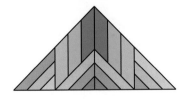

Block 4 — make 1

Quilt Assembly

Lay out the blocks and setting triangle blocks in diagonal rows as shown in the quilt assembly diagram.

Sew the blocks and triangle blocks into rows. Sew the rows together.

Quilt and bind the quilt according to your favorite method.

Quilt assembly

PAINTED DESERT, 72" x 84", made by the author,
quilted by Jeanne Zyck, Leawood, Kansas

PAINTED DESERT

This quilt reminds me of a family vacation to California. We made several stops and one was in the Painted Desert. The colors remind me of the dunes in the distance, striated with gold and purples against the blue sky. Making the first border the same color as the setting triangles makes the blocks appear to float off the quilt.

Fabric Requirements

Group A—for the A/AR diamonds
- 1⅛ yards light gold
- 1⅛ yards medium gold/brown
- 1⅛ yards dark brown

Group B—for the B1 & B2 triangles
- ⅔ yard light blue
- 2⅛ yards medium blue for the blocks and border #3
- 1¼ yards dark blue for the A Blocks and binding

Group C—for the C1 & C2 triangles
- ⅔ yard light purple
- 1½ yards medium purple for the blocks and border #2
- ⅔ yard dark purple

Setting Triangles and Border #1
- 1¾ yards black

- 6 yards backing
- 80" x 92" batting

Strip-Sets and Cutting

Group A

Cut 30 strips 1¼" x WOF from each fabric in Group A.

Sew the strips into strip-sets in dark/medium/light order.

Following the Block Construction instructions (pages 13–16), cut 200 A/AR pairs.

Group B

Cut 24 strips 1" x WOF from each fabric in Group B.

Sew the strips into strip-sets in dark/medium/light order.

Cut 100 B1 and 100 B2 pairs.

Group C

Cut 24 strips 1" x WOF from each fabric in Group C.

Sew the strips into strip-sets in dark/medium/light order.

Cut 100 C1 and 100 C2 pairs.

Dark Blue

Cut 8 strips 2¼" x WOF for the binding.

Light Blue

Cut 8 strips 4½" x WOF for border #3.

Medium Purple

Cut 8 strips 2½" x WOF for border #2.

Black

Cut 2 strips 12½" x WOF. Cut 5 squares 12½" x 12½" and cut each on the diagonal twice to yield 18 side setting triangles.

Cut 1 strip 6½" x WOF. Cut 2 squares 6½" x 6½" and cut each on the diagonal once to yield 4 corner triangles.

Cut the remaining black fabric into 8 strips 2½" wide for border #1.

Block Assembly

Assemble the blocks as shown.

Block 1

Make 30 Block 1—the light stars.

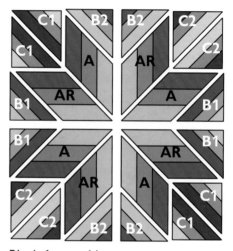

Block 1 assembly

Block 1 — make 30

BLOCK 2

Make 20 Block 2—the dark stars.

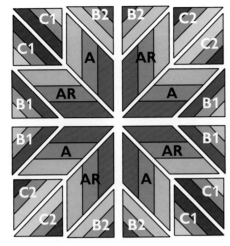

Block 2 assembly

Block 2 — make 20

Quilt Assembly

Lay out the blocks and setting triangles in diagonal rows as shown in the quilt assembly diagram.

Sew the blocks and triangles into rows. Sew the rows together.

Add the 3 borders.

Quilt and bind the quilt according to your favorite method.

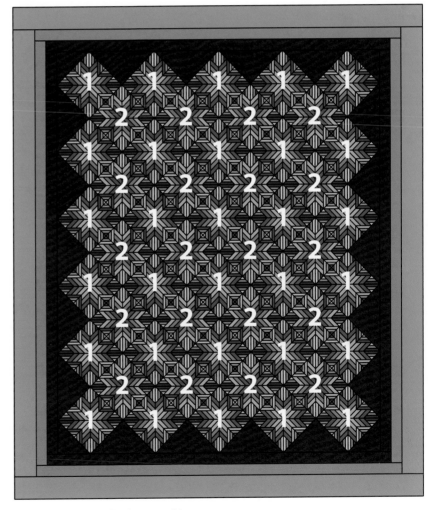

Quilt assembly

JULY SPARKLER, 48" x 60", made by the author,
quilted by Janiece Cline, Henderson, Nevada

July Sparkler

J ULY SPARKLER was the first quilt that I completed using this technique. The quilt uses a little extra fabric as you will only use the B1 and C2 cut pieces. The remaining triangles can be saved for another quilt (see page 29) or to make some accessories, like pillows or a table runner.

Fabric Requirements

Group A—for A diamonds
- ½ yard light cream print
- 1 yard medium cream (for the blocks and border #1)
- ½ yard dark cream tone-on-tone print

Group B—for the B1 & B2 triangles
- ⅝ yard light blue
- ⅝ yard medium blue
- 1½ yards dark blue (for the blocks and setting triangles)

Group C—for the C1 & C2 triangles
- ⅝ yard light red
- ⅝ yard medium red
- 2¼ yards dark red (for the blocks, border #2, and binding)

- 4 yards backing
- 56" x 68" batting

Strip-Sets and Cutting

GROUP A

Cut 10 strips 1¼" x WOF from each fabric in Group A.

Sew the strips into strip-sets in dark/medium/light order.

Following the Block Construction instructions (pages 13–16), cut 22 A pairs.

Cut 6 strips 2½" x WOF of medium cream for border #1.

GROUP B

Cut 20 strips 1" x WOF strips from each fabric in Group B.

Sew the strips into strip-sets in dark/medium/light order.

Cut 72 B1 pairs.

Set the B2 pairs aside and save for another project.

Cut 1 strip 14" x WOF of dark blue. Subcut into (3) 14" squares. Cut these squares twice on the diagonal for setting triangles.

Cut 2 squares 7¾" x 7¾" from the remaining strip. Cut these squares once on the diagonal for the corner triangles.

GROUP C

Cut 20 strips 1" x WOF strips from each fabric in Group C.

Sew the strips into strip-sets in dark/medium/light order.

Cut 72 C1 pairs.

Set the C2 pairs aside and save for another project.

Cut 8 strips 5½" x WOF of dark red for border #2.

Cut 7 strips 2¼" x WOF of dark red for the binding.

Block Assembly

Assemble the blocks as shown.

Make 18 Block 1.

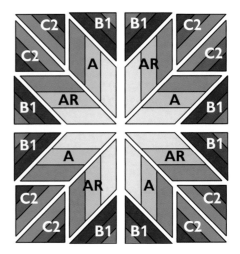

Block 1 assembly

Block 1 — make 18

Quilt Assembly

Lay out the blocks and setting triangles in diagonal rows as shown in the quilt assembly diagram.

Sew the blocks and triangles into rows. Sew the rows together.

Add border #1 and border #2.

Quilt and bind the quilt according to your favorite method.

Quilt assembly

Bonus Quilt:
July Sparkler II

You can make a second quilt with the leftover B2 and C1 triangles. Follow the assembly instructions for July Sparkler, substituting B2 and C1 for the B1 and C2 triangles.

Additional fabric needed:

Group A—star
- ½ yard light cream print
- 1 yard medium cream (for blocks and border #1)
- ½ yard dark cream tone-on-tone print

Group B
- 1 yard dark blue (setting triangles)

Group C
- 1⅝ yards dark red (for border #2 and binding)
- Backing—4 yards

12" Stars 'N Strips Block Projects

MOJAVE

Janiece made this version of MOJAVE without borders. She also changed the placement of the strips in the strip-sets. The strip-sets were pieced in light/stripy ikat/dark order.

above and opposite: **MOJAVE,** 51" x 69", made and quilted by Janiece Cline, Henderson, Nevada

Fabric Requirements

Group A—for the A/AR diamonds
- 2⅛ yard light rose
- 2½ yards red stripy ikat for the blocks and binding
- 2⅛ yard dark red

Group B—for the B1 & B2 triangles
- 1 yard light purple
- 1 yard purple stripy ikat
- 1 yard dark purple

Group C—for the C1 & C2 triangles
- 1 yard light blue
- 1 yard blue stripy ikat
- 1 yard dark blue

- 4½ yards backing
- 59" x 77" batting

Strip-Sets and Cutting

GROUP A

Cut 12 strips 1½" x WOF from each fabric in Group A.

Sew the strips into strip-sets in light/stripy ikat/dark order.

Following the Block Construction instructions (pages 13–16), cut 48 A/AR pairs.

GROUP B

Cut 14 strips 1¼" x WOF from each fabric in Group B.

Sew the strips into strip-sets in light/stripy ikat/dark order.

Cut 48 B1 and 49 B2 pairs.

GROUP C

Cut 14 strips 1¼" x WOF from each fabric in Group C.

Sew the strips into strip-sets in light/stripy ikat/dark order.

Cut 48 C1 and C2 pairs.

Block Assembly

Assemble the blocks as shown.

BLOCK 1

Make 12 Block 1.

* * * * * * * * * * *

BLOCK 2

Make 6 Block 2.

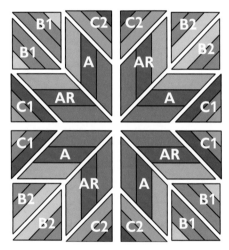

Block 1 assembly

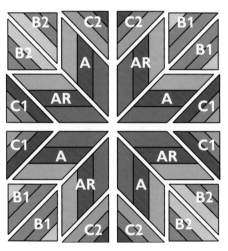

Block 2 assembly

Block 1 — make 12

Block 2 — make 6

Block 3

Make 6 Block 3—half blocks for the side setting triangles.

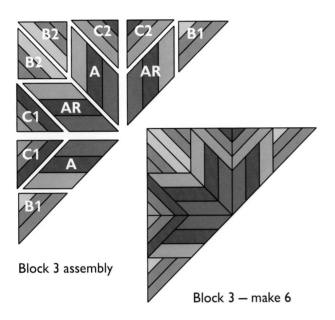

Block 3 assembly

Block 3 — make 6

Block 4

Make 4 Block 4—half blocks for the top and bottom setting triangles.

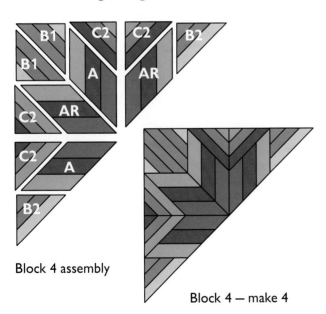

Block 4 assembly

Block 4 — make 4

Block 5

Make 2 Block 5—quarter blocks for the corner triangles.

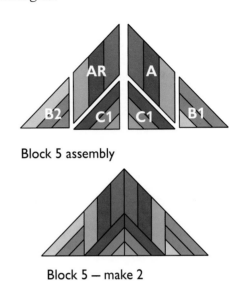

Block 5 assembly

Block 5 — make 2

* * * * * * * * * *

Block 6

Make 2 Block 6—the corner triangles.

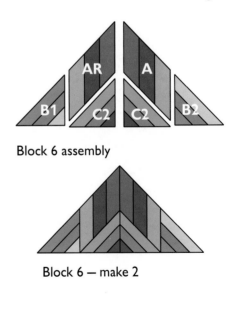

Block 6 assembly

Block 6 — make 2

Quilt Assembly

Lay out the blocks and setting triangles in diagonal rows as shown in the quilt assembly diagram.

Sew the blocks and triangles into rows. Sew the rows together.

Quilt and bind the quilt according to your favorite method.

Quilt assembly

MOJAVE SUNRISE, 40" x 54", made by the author,
quilted by Jeanne Zyck, Leawood, Kansas

Mojave Sunrise

T̲his quilt was inspired by another family trip, this time through the Mojave Desert. Still cool, the sun rises over the desert, and the sun's rays streak though the sky and warm the sand.

Fabric Requirements

Group A—for the A diamonds
- 1 yard light rose
- 1 yard red stripy ikat
- 1 yard dark red

Group B—for the B1 & B2 triangles
- ½ yard blue teal
- 2⅜ yards blue stripy ikat for the blocks, border, and bias-cut binding
- ½ yard dark teal

Group C—for the C1 & C2 triangles
- ½ yard light purple
- ½ yard purple stripy ikat
- ½ yard dark purple

- 5¼ yards backing
- 42" x 59" batting

Strip-Sets and Cutting

GROUP A

Cut 10 strips 1½" x WOF from each fabric in Group A.

Sew the strips into strip-sets in light/dark/stripy ikat order. When layering the strip-sets for cutting, position the stripy ikat closest to you.

Following the Block Construction instructions (pages 13–16), cut 48 A/AR pairs.

GROUP B

Cut 5 strips 6" wide of blue stripy ikat for the border.

Cut 14 strips 1¼" x WOF from each fabric in Group B.

Sew the strips into strip-sets in light/dark/stripy ikat order. When layering the strip-sets for cutting, position the stripy ikat closest to you.

Cut 48 B1 and 49 B2 pairs.

GROUP C

Cut 14 strips 1¼" x WOF from each fabric in Group B.

Sew the strips into strip-sets in light/dark/stripy ikat order. When layering the strip-sets for cutting, position the stripy ikat closest to you.

Cut 48 C1 and 48 C2 pairs.

Block Assembly

Assemble the blocks as shown.

BLOCK 1

Make 6 Block 1.

* * * * * * * * * *

BLOCK 2

Make 2 Block 2.

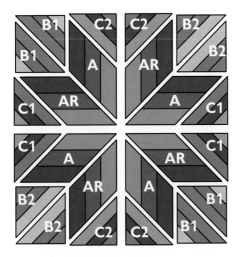

Block 1 assembly

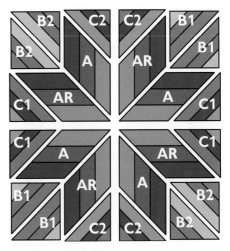

Block 2 assembly

Block 1 — make 6

Block 2 — make 2

Block 3

Make 4 Block 3—half blocks for the side setting triangles.

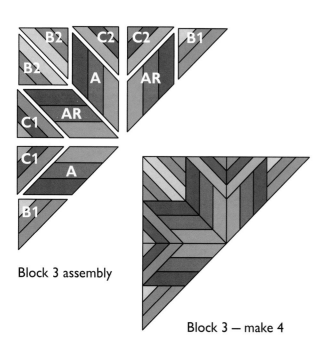

Block 3 assembly

Block 3 — make 4

Block 5

Make 2 Block 5—quarter blocks for the corner triangles.

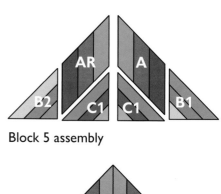

Block 5 assembly

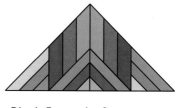

Block 5 — make 2

★ ★ ★ ★ ★ ★ ★ ★ ★ ★ ★

Block 6

Make 2 Block 6—quarter blocks for the corner triangles.

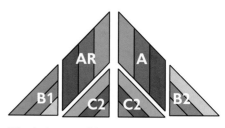

Block 6 assembly

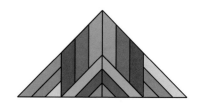

Block 6 — make 2

★ ★ ★ ★ ★ ★ ★ ★ ★ ★ ★

Block 4

Make 2 Block 4—half blocks for the top and bottom setting triangles.

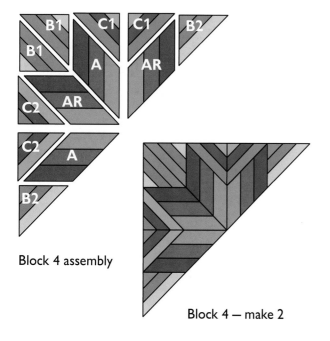

Block 4 assembly

Block 4 — make 2

Quilt Assembly

Lay out the blocks and setting triangles in diagonal rows as shown in the quilt assembly diagram.

Sew the blocks and triangles into rows. Sew the rows together.

Add the border.

Quilt and bind the quilt according to your favorite method.

Quilt assembly

MOJAVE SUNSET, 60" x 84", made by the author,
quilted by Jeanne Zyck, Leawood, Kansas

MOJAVE SUNSET

The sunset in the desert is hot and bright. After a long day of warming in the sun, the sand and air are hot and the colors of the desert pop!

Fabric Requirements

Group A—for the A/AR diamonds
- 1 yard light rose
- 2⅞ yards red stripy ikat for the blocks, border, and bias-cut binding
- 1 yard dark red

Group B—for the B1 & B2 triangles
- ½ yard blue teal
- ½ yard blue stripy ikat
- ½ yard dark teal

Group C—for the C1 & C2 triangles
- ½ yard light purple
- ½ yard purple stripy ikat
- ½ yard dark purple

- 5¼ yards backing
- 71" x 88" batting

Strip-Sets and Cutting

GROUP A

Cut 7 strips 6" wide of the red stripy ikat for the border.

Cut 10 strips 1½" x WOF from each fabric in Group A.

Sew the strips into strip-sets in light/dark/stripy ikat order.

Following the Block Construction instructions (pages 13–16), cut 48 A/AR pairs.

GROUP B

Cut 14 strips 1¼" x WOF from each fabric in Group B.

Sew the strips into strip-sets in light/dark/stripy ikat order.

Cut 48 B1 and 49 B2 pairs.

GROUP C

Cut 14 strips 1¼" x WOF from each fabric in Group B.

Sew the strips into strip-sets in light/dark/stripy ikat order.

Cut 48 C1 and C2 pairs.

Block Assembly

Assemble the blocks as shown.

Block 1

Make 6 Block 1.

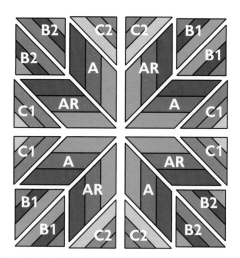

Block 2 assembly

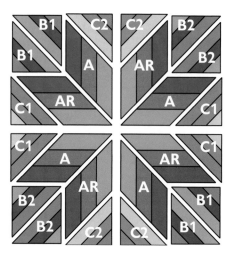

Block 1 assembly

Block 2 — make 2

Block 1 — make 6

* * * * * * * * * *

Block 2

Make 2 Block 2.

* * * * * * * * * *

Block 3

Make 4 Block 3.

* * * * * * * * * *

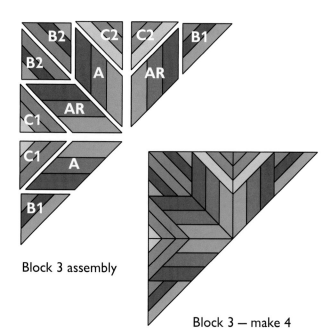

Block 3 assembly

Block 3 — make 4

BLOCK 4

Make 2 Block 4.

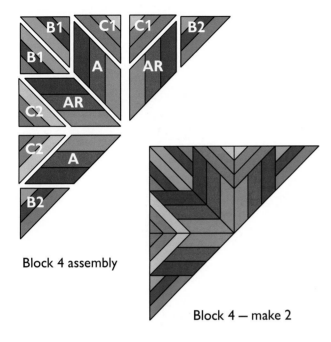

Block 4 assembly

Block 4 — make 2

* * * * * * * * * * *

BLOCK 5

Make 2 Block 5.

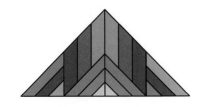

Block 5 assembly

Block 5 — make 2

BLOCK 6

Make 2 Block 6.

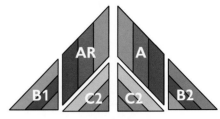

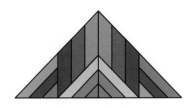

Block 6 assembly

Block 6 — make 2

Quilt Assembly

Lay out the blocks in diagonal rows as shown in the quilt assembly diagram (page 44).

Sew the blocks into rows. Sew the rows together.

Add the border.

Quilt and bind the quilt according to your favorite method.

Quilt assembly

CHRISTMAS JEWEL, 55" x 67", made by the author,
quilted by Janiece Cline, Henderson, Nevada

CHRISTMAS JEWEL

This quilt reminds me of the traditional family Christmases we enjoyed as I was growing up. The colors and fabric remind me of everything the holiday has to offer.

Fabric Requirements

Group A—for the A/AR diamonds
- ⅞ yard light red cotton
- ⅞ yard medium red silk
- 1¼ yards dark red cotton for the blocks and binding

Group B—for the B1 & B2 triangles
- ⅝ yard cream silk
- ⅝ yard medium gold metallic cotton
- ⅝ yard dark gold cotton satin
- ⅝ yard medium gold cotton for border #2

Group C—for the C1 & C2 triangles
- ⅝ yard light green cotton
- ⅝ yard medium green silk
- ⅝ yard dark green cotton satin
- ⅝ yard light green cotton for border #1

- 5¼ yards backing
- 63" x 75" batting

Strip-Sets and Cutting

GROUP A
Cut 12 strips 1½" x WOF from each fabric in Group A.

Sew the strips into strip-sets in dark/medium/light order.

Following the Block Construction instructions (pages 13–16), cut 80 A/AR pairs.

GROUP B
Cut 14 strips 1¼" x WOF from each fabric in Group B.

Sew the strips into strip-sets in dark/medium/light order.

Cut 40 B1 and 40 B2 pairs.

GROUP C
Cut 14 strips 1¼" x WOF from each fabric in Group B.

Sew the strips into strip-sets in dark/medium/light order.

Cut 40 C1 and 40 C2 pairs.

BORDERS AND BINDING

Cut the remaining green silk into 6 strips 1½" x WOF for border #1.

Cut the remaining cream metallic print into 6 strips 2½" x WOF for border #2.

Cut the remaining dark red into 7 strips 2¼" wide for the binding.

Block Assembly

Assemble the blocks as shown.

Make 20 Block 1.

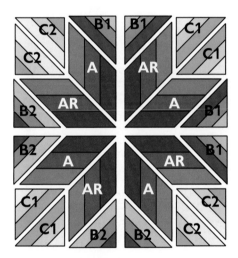

Block 1 assembly

Block 1 — make 20

Quilt Assembly

Lay out the blocks in 5 rows of 4 blocks each as shown in the quilt assembly diagram.

Sew the blocks into rows. Sew the rows together.

Add border #1 and border #2.

Quilt and bind the quilt according to your favorite method.

Quilt assembly

CUTTING CORNERS, 34" x 51", made by the author,
quilted by Jeanne Zyck, Leawood, Kansas

CUTTING CORNERS

This quilt uses only three colors, giving it a graphic quality. Choose bright colors for a lively look. It's great as a kid's quilt or a lap robe for those chilly nights. Sew the strips in dark/light/medium order.

Fabric Requirements
- ⅞ yard strawberry
- 1¼ yards grape for the blocks and binding
- ⅞ yard tangerine

- 1¾ yards backing
- 40" x 57" batting

Strips Sets and Cutting

GROUP A—for the A/AR diamonds

Cut 8 strips 1½" x WOF from each fabric.

Sew the strips into strip-sets in dark/light/medium order.

Following the Block Construction instructions (pages 13–16), cut 44 A pairs.

GROUP B—for the B1 & B2 triangles

Cut 14 strips 1¼" x WOF from each fabric.

Sew the strips into strip-sets in dark/light/medium order.

Cut 44 B1 and 44 B2 pairs.

BINDING

Cut 5 strips 2¼" from the grape.

Block Assembly

Assemble the blocks as shown.

Block 1

Make 6 Block 1.

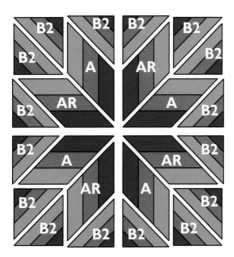

Block 1 assembly

Block 1 — make 6

* * * * * * * * * * * *

Block 2

Make 2 Block 2.

* * * * * * * * * * * *

Block 3

Make 6 Block 3—half blocks for the setting triangles.

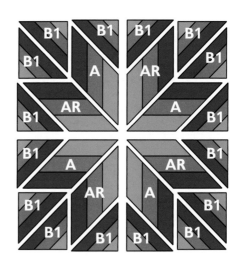

Block 2 assembly

Block 2 — make 2

* * * * * * * * * *

Block 3 assembly

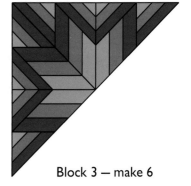

Block 3 — make 6

Quilt Assembly

Lay out the blocks and setting triangles in diagonal rows as shown in the quilt assembly diagram.

Sew the blocks and triangles into rows. Sew the rows together.

Quilt and bind the quilt according to your favorite method.

Quilt assembly

This Way That Way, 34" x 51", made by the author,
quilted by Jeanne Zyck, Leawood, Kansas

THIS WAY THAT WAY

This quilt has the same three colors as CUTTING CORNERS. Just by rearranging the order of the strips in the strip-sets, you get a totally different look. The strip-sets are sewn in medium/dark/light order.

Fabric Requirements

- ⅞ yard strawberry
- 1¼ yards grape for the blocks and binding
- ⅞ yard tangerine

- 1¾ yards backing
- 40" x 59" batting

Strip-Sets and Cutting

GROUP A—for the A/AR diamonds

Cut 8 strips 1½" x WOF from each fabric.

Sew the strips into strip-sets in medium/dark/light order.

Following the Block Construction instructions (pages 13–16), cut 44 A/AR pairs.

GROUP B—for the B1 & B2 triangles

Cut 14 strips 1¼" x WOF from each fabric.

Sew the strips into strip-sets in medium/dark/light order.

Cut 44 B1 and 44 B2 pairs.

BINDING

Cut 5 strips 2¼" from grape for the binding.

Block Assembly

Assemble the blocks as shown.

Block 1

Make 8 Block 1.

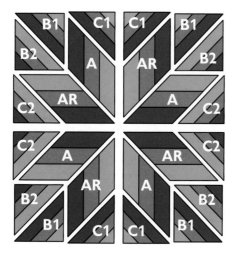

Block 1 assembly

Block 1 — make 8

Block 2

Make 4 Block 2—half blocks for the side setting triangles.

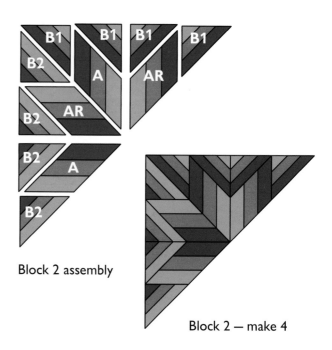

Block 2 assembly

Block 2 — make 4

* * * * * * * * * * *

Block 3

Make 2 Block 3—half blocks for the top and bottom setting triangles.

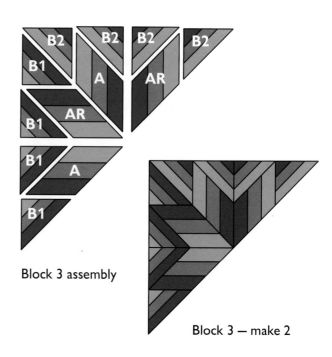

Block 3 assembly

Block 3 — make 2

Quilt Assembly

Lay out the blocks and setting triangles in diagonal rows as shown in the quilt assembly diagram.

Sew the blocks and triangles into rows. Sew the rows together.

Quilt and bind the quilt according to your favorite method.

Quilt assembly

Stars 'N Strips Block Variations

City Nights
(18" Block)

In the city surrounded by tall buildings, the sunlight shines between and glistens off of the many windows. This is a variation on the standard Stars 'N Strips block with 2 diamond pieces (A & B) and 1 set of triangles (C).

You will have enough blocks left over to complete the CITY BLOCKS quilt (pages 62–65).

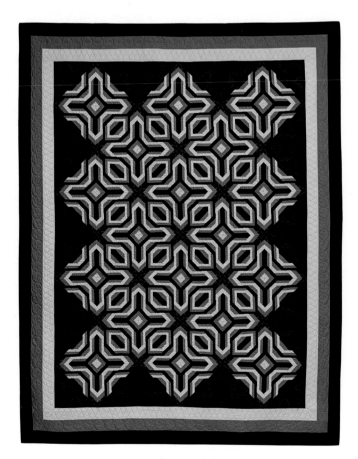

opposite and above: **CITY NIGHTS**, 80" x 102", made by the author, quilted by Janiece Cline, Henderson, Nevada

Fabric Requirements

- 7⅝ yards black for the blocks, setting triangles, border #3, and binding
- 4¾ yards dark gray for the blocks and border #2
- 4¾ yards light gray for the blocks and border #1

- 10½ yards backing
- 88" x 110" batting

Strip-Sets and Cutting

PIECE A

Cut 12 strips 1⅜" x WOF from each color.

Sew the strips into strip-sets.

Following the Block Construction instructions (pages 13–16), cut 72 A/AR diamond pair segments 2⅛" wide. Cut 144 B/BR diamond pair segments 3¼" wide.

PIECE B

Cut 32 strips 1⅛" x WOF from each color.

Sew the strips into strip-sets.

Cut 144 D/DR diamond pair segments 3¼" wide.

PIECE C

Cut 80 strips 1⅛" x WOF from each color.

Sew the strips into strip-sets.

Use the Easy Angle™ tool by Sharon Hultgren to cut half-square triangles from 2 strip-sets placed right sides together.

Line up the 4½" line with the middle strip seamline and cut along both sides of the ruler.

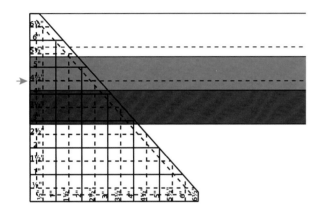

Flip your ruler over, lining up the 4½" line now with the light gray seamline and the angled edge along the cut edge.

Cut along the straight edge of the ruler.

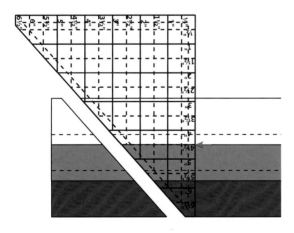

You will now have two pairs.

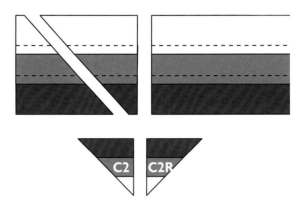

Cut 216 pairs of Piece C1/C1R triangles and 216 pairs of C2/C2R triangles.

Set aside the C2/C2R triangles for the CITY BLOCKS quilt (pages 62-65).

SETTING TRIANGLES AND BORDERS

Cut 2 strips 23⅞" x WOF from the black. Cut 3 squares 23⅞" x 23⅞". Cut twice on the diagonal for the side setting triangles. (You'll only use 10.)

Cut 1 strip 12⅛" x WOF. Cut 2 squares 12⅛" x 12⅛". Cut once on the diagonal for the corner triangles.

Cut 8 strips 2½" x WOF from each color for the borders.

Cut 9 strips 2¼" x WOF from the black for the binding.

Block Assembly

1. Piece section 1.

Join B & C1.

2.

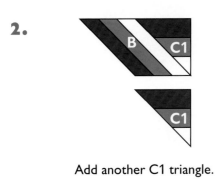

Add another C1 triangle.

3.

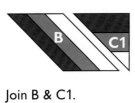

Completed section 1

4. Piece section 2.

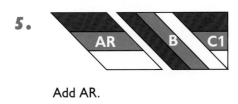

Join B & C1.

5.

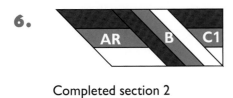

Add AR.

6.

Completed section 2

7.

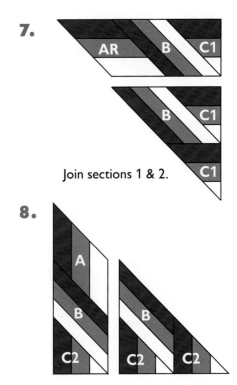

Join sections 1 & 2.

8.

Repeat these steps with the A, BR & C1R pieces.

9.

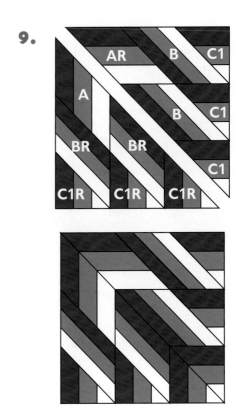

Sew the two sections together to complete one quarter of the block.

Sew 4 quarter sections together to complete the block. Make 18.

Quilt Assembly

Lay out the blocks and setting triangles in diagonal rows as shown in the quilt assembly diagram.

Sew the blocks and triangles into rows. Sew the rows together.

Add the 3 borders.

Quilt and bind the quilt according to your favorite method.

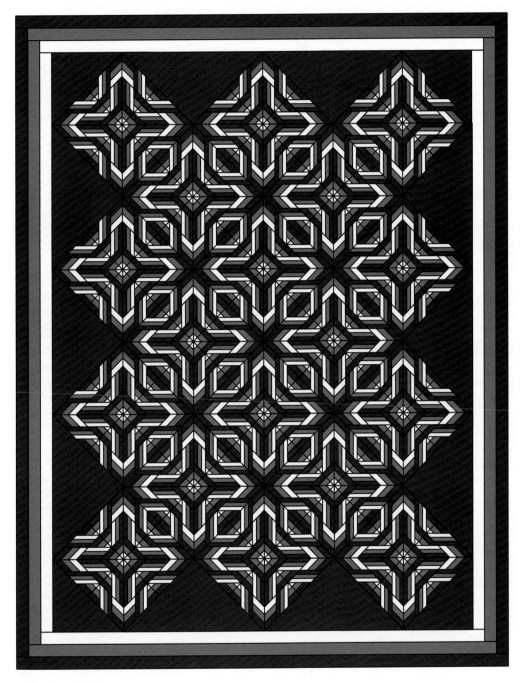

Quilt assembly

CITY BLOCKS, 64" x 74", made by the author

City Blocks
(7" Block)

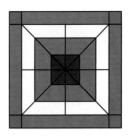

Create this quilt from the C2 & C2R triangles left over from making the City Nights quilt (pages 56–61).

Fabric Requirements

- 224 triangle pairs remaining from the City Nights project
- ⅛ yard solid red
- 1 yard solid dark gray
- ⅞ yard black for border #1 and binding
- 1⅝ yards red & black print for border #2

- 5 yards backing
- 72" x 82" batting

Cutting

Cut 3 strips 1¼" x WOF from the solid red.

Cut 4 strips 7½" x WOF from the solid dark gray.

Cut 8 strips 1¼" x WOF from the black for border #1.

Cut 7 strips 2¼" strips from the black for the binding.

Cut 8 strips 5" x WOF strips of the red & black print for border #2.

Assembly

Sew triangle pairs to create 224 quarter-square triangles.

Make 224 quarter-square triangles.

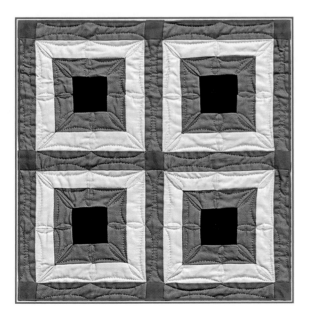

Join 2 quarter-square triangles into 112 half-square triangles.

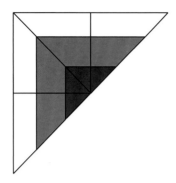

Make 112 half-square triangles.

Sew the half square triangles together to yield a 7½" x 7½" block. Make 56 blocks. Square up if necessary.

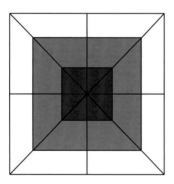

Make 56 blocks.

Cut 56 strips 7½" x 1¼" from the dark gray. Add the strips to one side of each block.

NOTE:
An alternative method would be to chain piece the blocks onto the gray strips, then trim.

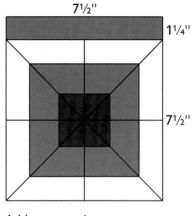

7½"

1¼"

7½"

Add a gray strip.

Make 2 strips-sets, each with a red 1¼" strip and a 7½" dark gray strip. Cut 56 1¼" rectangles from the strip-sets.

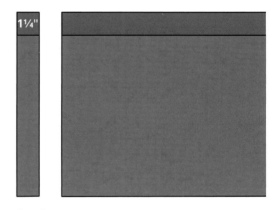

1¼"

Cut 56 red/gray units.

Sew a red/grey unit to the right side of all the blocks.

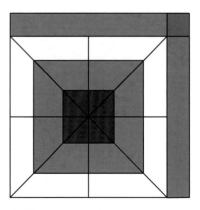

Add to the blocks.

Lay out the blocks in 8 rows of 7 blocks each.

Sew a red/gray unit to the left side of the 8 blocks along the left side of the layout.

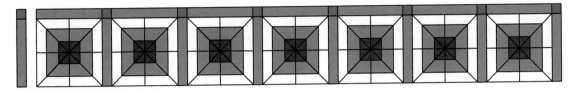

Add to 8 blocks

Sew a red/gray unit to the bottom of the block in the lower right corner of the layout.

Cut 7 squares 1¼" x 1¼" from the remaining solid red strip. Sew this square to the opposite end of the 7 remaining red/gray units. Sew this unit to the bottom of the rest of the bottom row of blocks.

Quilt Assembly

Sew the blocks into rows and then sew the rows together.

Add black border #1, then the red & black print border #2.

Quilt and bind the quilt according to your favorite method.

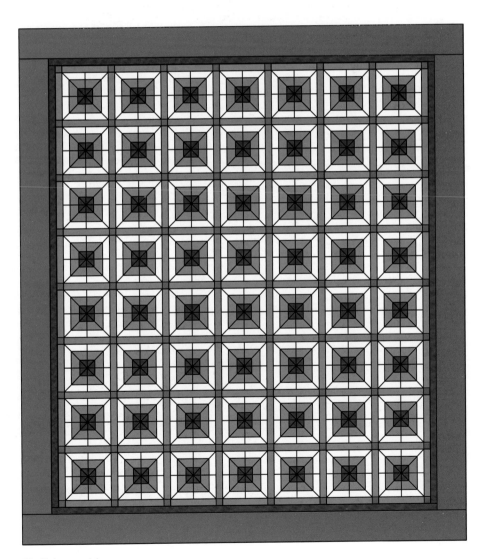

Quilt assembly

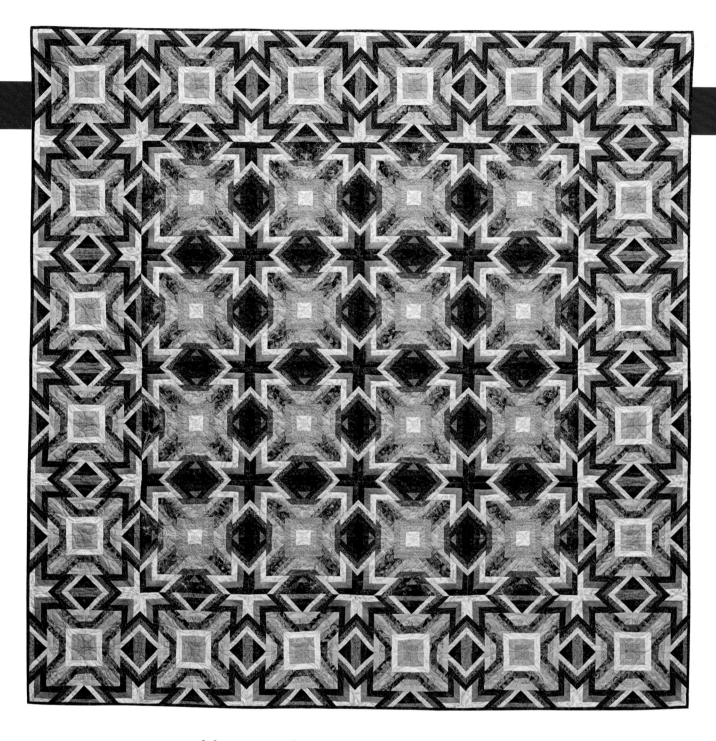

MORNING GLORY, 72" x 72" made by the author,
quilted by Janiece Cline, Henderson, Nevada

Morning Glory
(12" Block)

Every day during the summer I see morning glories climbing a trellis.

Fabric Requirements

Group A
- 1 yard each of a light, medium, and dark mauve (3 yards total)

Group B
- 1 yard each of a light, medium, and dark blue (3 yards total)

Groups C
- 1 yard each of a light, medium, and dark blue-green (3 yards total)

Group D
- 1 yard each of a light, medium, and dark purple (3 yards total)

Group E
- 1 yard each of a light, medium, and dark green (3 yards total)

Group F
- 1 yard each of dark brown, light brown, and cream (3 yards total)

- ½ yard binding
- 8 yards backing
- 80" x 80" batting

Strip-Sets and Cutting

GROUP A, B, AND C

Cut 28 strips 1⅛" x WOF from the light, medium, and dark in each colorway.

Sew the strips into strip-sets in dark/medium/light order.

Layer two strip-sets right sides together, each with the darkest strip nearest you. Using the Easy Angle, line up the bottom of the strip-set with the 4" line. With a rotary cutter, cut on both sides of the ruler (Piece 1). Flip the ruler over and line the top of the strip-set with the 4" line. Cut alongside the ruler again (Piece 2).

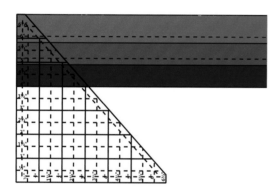

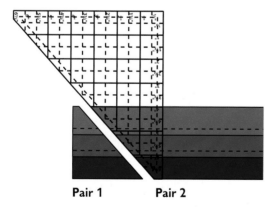

Pair 1   Pair 2

Cutting C triangles

You will need the following number of pairs for each colorway:

64 A1, B1, and C1 pairs

80 of A2, B2, and C2 pairs

GROUP D/DR AND E/ER

Cut 36 strips 1" x WOF from the light, medium, and dark in each colorway.

Sew the strips into strip-sets in dark/medium/light order.

Arrange two strip-sets as before and cut 144 diamond pairs 2½" wide from each colorway.

GROUP F/FR

Cut 28 strips 1⅛" x WOF from each F fabric.

Sew the strips into strip-sets in dark/medium/light order.

Arrange two strip-sets as before and cut 144 diamond pairs 1⅞" wide.

Block Assembly

Follow the piecing sequence of the blocks in the CITY NIGHTS pattern (pages 56–61) to assemble the blocks as follows:

BLOCK 1

Make 16 Block 1.

1.

Piecing section 1

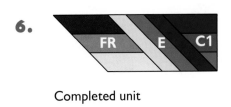

6.

Completed unit

NOTE:

The darks in Piece D meet in the middle. The dark of Piece E is closest to the C1 triangle. The dark of Piece E is on the outside of the block.

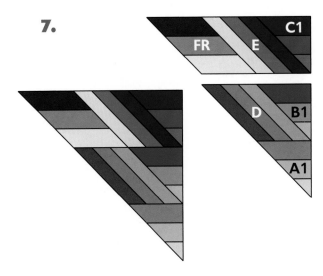

7.

Finishing up the next portions

2.

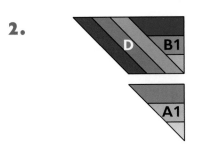

Piecing section 2

3.

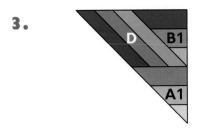

Join sections 1 & 2.

8.

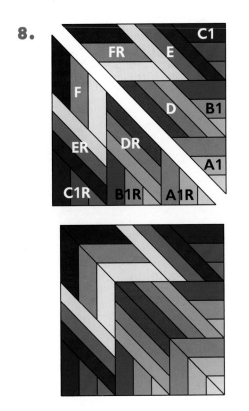

4.

Join the E & C1 pieces.

5.

Add an FR piece.

Sew the two sections together to complete one quarter of the block.

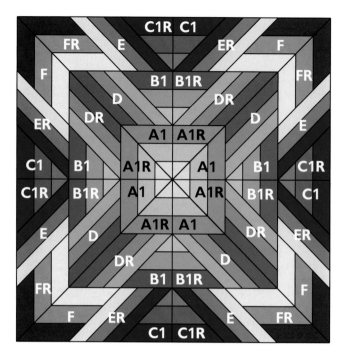

Sew 4 quarter sections together to complete the block. Make 16.

* * * * * * * * * * *

BLOCK 2

Make 20 Block 2.

NOTE:

Pieces D, E, and F are positioned opposite of how they are positioned in Block 1.

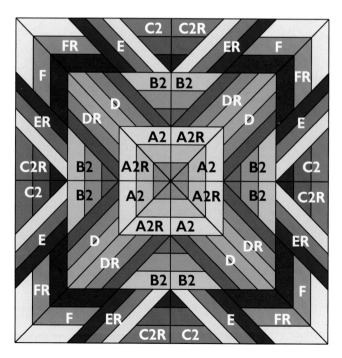

Block 2 — make 20.

Final Assembly

Lay out the blocks and setting triangles in diagonal rows as shown in the quilt assembly diagram.

Sew the blocks and triangles into rows. Sew the rows together.

Quilt and bind the quilt according to your favorite method.

Quilt assembly

Additional Projects

PILLOWS

I used my leftover pieces to create a pillow top. If you are using a pillow form, add borders to your block to make it the correct size. Bind as you would any quilt for a "fake" piping.

opposite: MOJAVE SUNSET, detail, full quilt on page 40

below: Leftovers from MOJAVE SUNSET were used to make this pillow top.

above: **Leftovers from** MOJAVE SUNRISE **were used to make this pillow top.**

opposite: MOJAVE SUNRISE, **detail, full quilt on page 35**

above and right: **Leftovers from** CHRISTMAS JEWEL **were used to make these pillow tops.**

opposite: CHRISTMAS JEWEL, detail, full quilt on page 45

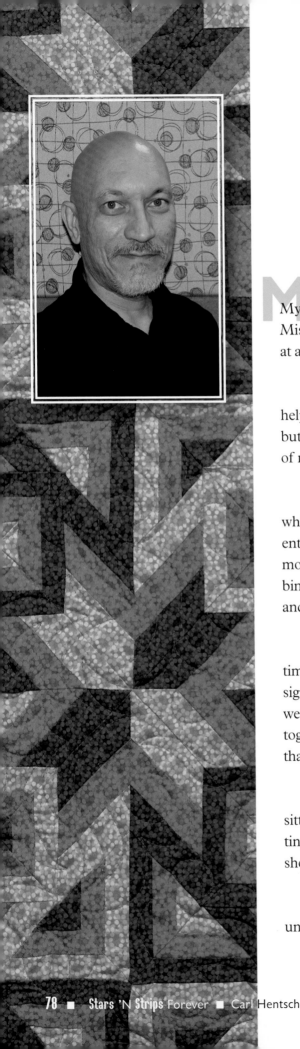

Meet Carl Hentsch

My recent quilting adventures reemerged when I moved to Missouri around 2006. However, my interest in crafting started at a very young age. I began my first craft project at the age of ten.

My first niece was about to be born and, with my mother's help, I created a quilt for her. Now this was not a patchwork quilt, but was hand embroidered. I carefully selected pages from many of my coloring books.

My mother then transferred the images to a piece of fabric, which I then embroidered with a running stitch. I used different colored threads and colored in each area with crayons. My mother heat-set the color and we completed it with a backing and binding. My niece used that blanket until it was tattered and torn, and even then she still carried it around in her pillowcase.

As my niece grew, so did my craft and design sense. By the time she was walking I was designing dresses for her. After I designed a dress, my mother again was there to help me. Together we created a pattern, cut out the fabric, and then she sewed it all together. How great it felt to have my niece wearing something that I helped to create!

Needless to say, my interests also grew. I remember one year sitting around while my aunt visited from Chicago. She was knitting Christmas bells and I was totally enthralled. I asked her to show me and I learned to knit at an early age.

Many years went by. I graduated from high school and the university and joined the Air Force. It was during my time in the

Air Force, probably around 1990, that one of my friends was knitting booties, and I remembered, "Hey, I can do that, too." I immediately drove to the nearest yarn shop, bought a book, yarn, and needles, and proceeded to knit a cabled sweater. Unbelievably, the sweater was completed *and wearable!* So, I continued to knit and knit and knit!

You must be thinking to yourself, "So, when did he actually start quilting?" To answer that, we would have to fast forward to the mid to late 90's. I discovered HGTV and Alex Anderson. Oh, what was that she was doing? Cutting up fabric and sewing it back together and making a quilt? Oh, wait, now there was PBS and Eleanor Burns' *Quilt in a Day.* I watched many shows, thinking to myself, "I wish I could do that." I bought some magazines and continued to watch the programs. Then one day, there was Eleanor's son on the show and he was quilting! Wow, guys can do it too!

After that, I knew I had to try. I headed to my nearest Hancock Fabrics store (there were not quilt shops that I knew of in Florida at the time) and bought a pattern, fabric, and all the necessary rotary cutting tools. I proceeded to measure, cut, sew, and then quilt my handiwork. After see-

ing that mess, I am amazed that I tried again. I tried one or two more projects with little to no success. Then I found it! A quilt-as-you-go Log Cabin book. How great, how simple! I am sure it would have been, had I not selected the thickest polyester batting made! I did complete the quilt, but after the first few washings, the seams began to burst. What a mess!

But I wasn't going to give up! By this time Alex Anderson had a few male quilters on her program. "By gosh, if they can do it, so can I!"

My next attempt was a block-of-the-month around 2001. I figured if I took my time, I might be able to make this work. By this time, two quilt shops had opened near my small town in Florida. I bought the fabric and, wouldn't you know, after 12 months, I had my first completed quilt! I took it to a local quilter and I still have that quilt today.

After my mother passed away, I stopped quilting, moved around a bit, and then finally settled in Saint Joseph, Missouri, in 2006. It was here I rediscovered my love of quilting, found wonderful quilt shops, and the rest, as they say, is history.

more AQS Books

This is only a small selection of the books available from the American Quilter's Society. AQS books are known worldwide for timely topics, clear writing, beautiful color photos, and accurate illustrations and patterns. The following books are available from your local bookseller, quilt shop, or public library.

#8671

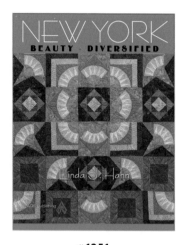

#1251

#8663

#8664

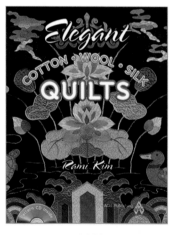

#8681

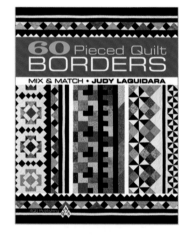

#8662

#8529

#8532

#8146